Investigating
Why It Rains

Ellen René

PowerKiDS
press.
New York

To my father, who loved rainy "s & s" days

Published in 2009 by The Rosen Publishing Group, Inc.
29 East 21st Street, New York, NY 10010

First Edition

Editor: Joanne Randolph
Book Design: Julio Gil
Photo Researcher: Jessica Gerweck

Photo Credits: Cover, back cover (middle right) © Fat Chance Productions; back cover (top center, top right, middle left, bottom left), pp. 5, 6, 10, 13, 14, 17, 18, 21 Shutterstock; back cover (middle center) © Jim Merli; p. 9 by Greg Tucker.

Library of Congress Cataloging-in-Publication Data

René, Ellen.
  Investigating why it rains / Ellen René. — 1st ed.
      p. cm. — (Science detectives)
  Includes index.
  ISBN 978-1-4042-4483-2 (library binding)
  1. Rain and rainfall—Juvenile literature. 2. Hydrologic cycle—Juvenile literature. I. Title.
  QC924.7.R46 2009
  551.57'7—dc22
                                            2008001091

Manufactured in the United States of America

Contents

Rain, Rain Go Away

Have you ever wished it would stop raining? Maybe you had to play inside during recess. Maybe your soccer game or trip to the beach got called off. Rain washes out more than fun and games. Too much rain floods roads and houses. Too little rain dries up crops and soil, though.

We cannot control the weather. It helps to prepare for it, though. All our weather happens in the **atmosphere**, the blanket of air covering Earth. **Meteorologists** study the atmosphere to **predict** where, when, and how much it will rain. What clues do these weather scientists look for?

Rain may seem like no fun, but if you think like a scientist, you may learn some interesting things about rain. What do you want to know?

Water is everywhere, even inside living things. People must drink a lot of water to put back the water we lose breathing and sweating.

Water, Water Everywhere

First it is important to understand where the water that falls as rain comes from. Oceans cover large parts of Earth. They hold most of its water. Lakes, rivers, and streams store water, too. Soil does as well. Water is locked in glaciers, ice caps, and snowfields. It is held in the atmosphere as a gas, called **water vapor**.

Earth's water is used over and over again. It moves from oceans, to air, to land, and back to oceans. As it does this, it changes forms, from water, to water vapor, to ice, and back again. Rain plays an important part in this **cycle**.

What Is the Water Cycle?

Did you know that the water in your bathtub is very, very old? Even if it fell as rain a short time ago, the water was around when dinosaurs walked on Earth.

All the water on Earth is part of a never-ending water cycle. Understanding how the water cycle works will bring us another step closer to understanding why it rains.

The Sun powers this cycle. It heats the water on Earth. This causes some of the water to **evaporate**, or change into a gas. The gas, called water vapor, then rises into the atmosphere. As it rises, it cools and **condenses**. This means it changes from a gas back into water. It forms clouds. Rain and other types of **precipitation** fall from the clouds. This returns water to Earth.

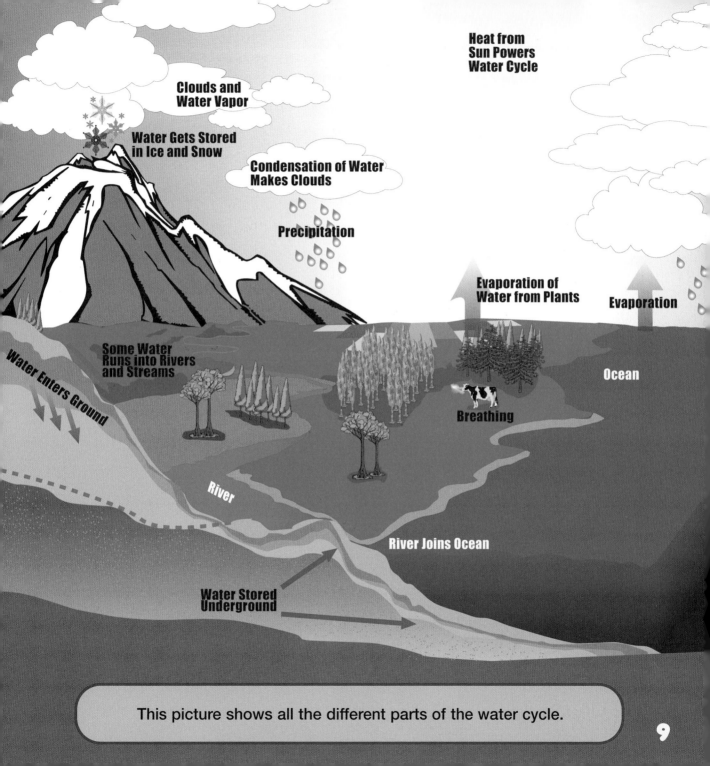

This picture shows all the different parts of the water cycle.

These buffalo put water back into the air as they breathe. The water plants and animals give off becomes part of the water cycle, too.

More About Evaporation

A key part of the water cycle is evaporation. You cannot see evaporation. You may have felt it, though. Have you ever been cold when you came out of a swimming pool? As water evaporated from your skin into the air, it cooled you. The same thing happens when you sweat. Your sweat is part of the water cycle.

Evaporation adds water vapor to the atmosphere. Most water in the atmosphere has evaporated from Earth's oceans. Rainfall puts back some of the water that was lost but not all of it. The oceans do not dry up, though. Can you guess why? The ocean gets water from rivers and underground places, too.

More About Condensation

Do you know that you can make a cloud? Just breathe out through your mouth on a very cold day. When warm, moist air from your body mixes with cold air, a cloud forms. Then you can see your breath.

Changing water vapor back into water is called condensation. Condensation forms clouds. How does that work? Have you ever held a glass filled with lemonade and ice? Did drops form on the outside? Where did they come from? They came from the air.

Warm air holds more water vapor than cold air. When air cools, it cannot hold all its **moisture**. Water comes out. When water vapor in the warmer air hits your icy glass, it changes back to water as it cools. Clouds form when warm air cools and cannot hold all its moisture.

Have you ever seen drops of water on the grass in the morning?
This is called dew, which forms by condensation.

In the darker part of this cloud, a lot of droplets have come together. Soon they will fall as rain.

What Happens Inside a Cloud?

How does the water vapor in clouds end up as rain? Water vapor condenses on dust, salt, or smoke in the air. Tiny water droplets or ice **crystals** form. They are very light. Some need to get a hundred thousand times heavier before they fall. How do they get bigger?

Droplets grow when more water vapor condenses on them. They also grow by crashing into each other and joining together. Droplets swirl around in clouds and grow at different speeds. Scientists are still learning exactly how this happens. Some drops evaporate and become water vapor again. Some get so heavy they cannot stay in the air anymore.

It's Raining, It's Pouring!

The wettest place in the world is Tutunendo, Colombia. It gets around 463.4 inches (1,177 cm) of rain each year. Mount Waialeale, in Hawaii, has the most rainy days each year, about 350.

Rain is precipitation that reaches the ground as water. Many raindrops start out as snow or ice. They melt along the way as they pass through warmer air. Tiny drops that fall close together are called drizzle. Fifty drizzle drops side by side measure about 1 inch (2.5 cm). Bigger drops that do not fall so close together are called rain.

Some people think that raindrops are shaped like tears. They are not. Small drops are shaped like peas. Midsized drops are shaped like sandwich buns. Large drops are shaped like lima beans.

Here you can see small pea-shaped raindrops. You can see larger bun-shaped and lima-bean-shaped drops, too.

If you saw these clouds while you were out playing, you would know it was time to head inside. These are storm clouds.

Cloud Clues

Are you a cloud watcher? Do you watch clouds change shape? Do you hunt for ones that look like animals? Scientists watch clouds grow and change, too. Changing cloud shapes are clues to what is happening inside the clouds.

Clouds help scientists predict the weather. Wispy cirrus clouds form high in the sky. They are made of ice and point to a change in the weather. Gray stratus clouds form closer to the ground. They bring rain and drizzle. Puffy cumulus clouds are fair-weather clouds. They can become huge storm clouds that bring rain, snow, and **hail**, though.

Hail, Sleet, and Snow

Many clouds form every day. Few produce precipitation, though. What makes precipitation fall then? Hail forms when powerful winds toss icy drops up and down in a thundercloud. Water coats them and then turns to ice. They grow layer by layer like an onion, then crash to Earth. **Sleet** is rain that freezes when it passes through cold air near the ground. Snow forms from ice crystals that reach the ground without melting.

All precipitation returns water to Earth. Rain plays the biggest part in the water cycle. It is the main way water from the atmosphere gets back to Earth.

Snow falls instead of rain when it is very cold. Did you know that 1 inch (2.5 cm) of rain would make about 10 inches (25 cm) of snow?

Around and Around

More water falls on the land than evaporates from it. Some goes into the soil, where plants use it. Some ends up in streams and rivers, which flow to the ocean. Some falls into openings in Earth's crust and moves underground to the ocean.

This completes the cycle from ocean, to air, to land, and back to the ocean. It goes around and around and never stops. All living things need water. The water cycle makes life on Earth possible. Now, do you really wish it would stop raining?

Glossary

atmosphere (AT-muh-sfeer) The gases around an object in space. On Earth this is air.

condenses (kun-DENT-sez) Turns into drops of liquid, like water.

crystals (KRIS-tulz) Hard, clear things that have points and flat sides.

cycle (SY-kul) Actions that happen in the same order over and over.

evaporate (ih-VA-puh-rayt) To change from a liquid, such as water, to a gas.

hail (HAYL) Small pieces of ice that fall from the clouds.

meteorologists (mee-tee-uh-RAH-luh-jists) People who study the weather.

moisture (MOIS-chur) Small bits of water in the air.

precipitation (preh-sih-pih-TAY-shun) Any moisture that falls from the sky. Rain and snow are precipitation.

predict (prih-DIKT) To make a guess based on facts or knowledge.

sleet (SLEET) Icy rain.

water vapor (WAH-ter VAY-pur) The gaseous state of water.

Index

Web Sites

Due to the changing nature of Internet links, PowerKids Press has developed an online list of Web sites related to the subject of this book. This site is updated regularly. Please use this link to access the list:
www.powerkidslinks.com/scidet/whyrain/